Knights
& Castles

SIMON & SCHUSTER BOOKS FOR YOUNG READERS
An imprint of Simon & Schuster Children's Publishing Division
1230 Avenue of the Americas, New York, New York 10020

Conceived and produced by Weldon Owen Pty Ltd
61 Victoria Street, McMahons Point
Sydney, NSW 2060, Australia

Group Chief Executive Officer John Owen
President and Chief Executive Officer Terry Newell
Publisher Sheena Coupe
Creative Director Sue Burk
Concept Development John Bull, The Book Design Company
Editorial Coordinator Mike Crowton
Vice President, International Sales Stuart Laurence
Vice President, Sales and New Business Development Amy Kaneko
Vice President, Sales: Asia and Latin America Dawn Low
Administrator, International Sales Kristine Ravn

Project Editor Lachlan McLaine
Designer John Bull, The Book Design Company
Cover Designers Gaye Allen, Kelly Booth, and Brandi Valenza

Color reproduction by Chroma Graphics (Overseas) Pte Ltd
Printed by SNP Leefung Printers Ltd
Manufactured in China

A WELDON OWEN PRODUCTION

SIMON & SCHUSTER BOOKS FOR YOUNG READERS is a trademark of Simon & Schuster, Inc.
The text for this book is set in Meta and Rotis Serif.
10 9 8 7 6 5 4 3 2 1
Cataloging-in-publication data for this book is available from the Library of Congress.

ISBN-13: 978-1-4169-3864-4
ISBN-10: 1-4169-3864-8

Knights
& Castles

Philip Dixon

Simon & Schuster Books for Young Readers
New York London Toronto Sydney

Contents

 *focus*

A Knight's World

Castles

introducing

Knights of the
Middle Ages

For hundreds of years, knights were the most powerful soldiers and among the most important people in Europe. They were at their height for about 500 years in the Middle Ages (also called the medieval period), from 1000 to the 1500s. Society in the Middle Ages was like a pyramid. Each knight served a baron or earl, who, in turn, held his estates by giving loyalty and the service of his knights to the king. The first knights were just soldiers on horseback who served local lords. But the lords—who often had a lot of land but not much money— found it hard to keep the knights properly equipped. So they gave the knights land instead of supporting them. The knights became landlords, and the people on their land paid rent and worked for them.

The social pyramid

Almost everyone in medieval Europe lived by a strict social arrangement known as the feudal system. The king was at the top, the barons and their knights below, and the farmers and serfs at the bottom. All were connected by a complex system of rights and obligations, some of which are illustrated here.

The knight in shining armor
We often think of knights as romantic, adventurous figures always ready to ride to the rescue, and that is exactly how knights liked to think of themselves. This English drawing from the 1300s shows a knight slaying a dragon.

Cities and towns *Urban society was a miniature copy of the world outside the city walls: the mayor governed, with a council of rich traders (like barons), and the workmen and craftsmen paid them rents. Kings generally did not interfere, but they received payments for giving privileges.*

Barons *This class of nobles gave knights land. In return a knight swore loyalty to his baron and promised to help him in times of war. Barons often lived in fine castles.*

Knights *Some knights were mercenaries who fought simply for money, but most were given land by a baron in exchange for loyalty and service in battle. Unlike barons, the position of knight was not handed down from father to son.*

The king *No one individual today has anything like the power of a medieval king. He gave barons lands and privileges that they could pass on to their heirs. In exchange, barons gave the king loyalty and soldiers.*

The church *The greatest single landholder in Europe was the church, which owned nearly a third of the land. Its abbots and bishops were among the greatest of the barons. Church and state, headed by the king, were normally united since both required peace and prosperity.*

The pope *The pope was head of the church, and had to approve the appointment of bishops, abbots, and even kings. This sometimes led to bitter disputes, especially in the election of bishops.*

Bishops *These religious leaders were among the richest of the barons. They had their own knights and lands.*

Tithe *A tax of a tenth of food produced was owed by farmers each year to the church. The church used this wealth to pay salaries and maintain its buildings.*

Crusaders *When a knight or baron, or sometimes even the king, decided to go on crusade, his lands were protected and his rents were kept safe. He expected salvation through his action, especially if he died in the Holy Land.*

Farmers, laborers, and serfs *Most people lived and worked on land owned by knights and barons. In exchange they gave their labor and paid rent in cash or some of the food they produced. The majority were tied to the land and could not move away.*

Knights of the
Crusades

In the late 1000s, it became almost impossible for pilgrims to visit Jerusalem and the Holy Land in what is now Israel and Palestine. Therefore the pope called for a war to recapture the holy places from the Muslims who had controlled the area for more than 400 years. Men were encouraged to become crusaders with the promise that God would forgive their sins and that their rights at home would be protected while they were away. In the next 200 years, there were five great crusades. The crusaders captured Jerusalem and formed a Christian kingdom, but eventually the Muslims, under Saladin and later Sultan Baibars, drove the knights out and recaptured the holy cities.

Knights on a mission
Crusaders wore the same armor as at home, despite the heat of the Middle East. Most kept their own heraldry, but others banded together to form holy orders of fighting men and displayed the cross on their shields and surcoats.

Army on the march *Crusader armies lived off the land as they traveled. Many communities on the way to Jerusalem were devastated after thouands of hungry men had passed through.*

Longest journey
Some crusaders traveled from as far away as Ireland and Iceland.

Dangerous seas *Crusaders at sea were vulnerable to pirates, and many were sent as slaves to the kingdoms of the African coast.*

Stones they left behind
The castle of Sidon in Lebanon, built to safeguard the nearby harbor, is a good example of a crusader stronghold. The capture of castles such as this one in the 1200s marked the end of the crusader kingdoms.

King Louis sets sail

Saint Louis (King Louis IX of France) led two crusades, both of which ended in failure. In this drawing, he is shown embarking on his second crusade in 1270 from the port of Aigues Mortes in France.

Defenders of the east

The crusader knights fought many bloody battles against Muslim soldiers who were defending their land against invaders. These soldiers came from a number of different ethnic groups, but they formed an integrated army in response to the crusader threat.

Constantinople *Capital of the Byzantine Empire, Constantinople was the largest and wealthiest city in medieval Europe. The religion of the Byzantine Empire was the Greek Orthodox branch of Christianity.*

Crusader kingdoms *At their peak, the crusader kingdoms (the area colored purple) occupied present-day Israel, Palestine, western Syria, part of Jordan, and the Kurdish areas of Turkey and Armenia.*

Jerusalem *Holy to Jews, Christians, and Muslims, Jerusalem was the ultimate goal for Christian pilgrims. Once in control, the crusaders kept access open to the city for Christians alone.*

The journey to Jerusalem

Most crusaders came from the great kingdoms of Europe, such as England, France, and Germany, but troops came from all areas. The poor walked across to Constantinople (now called Istanbul, in Turkey), while the richer lords traveled by ship. Many crusaders never made it home again.

Knights and Soldiers
In Battle

Unlike modern armies, knights did not train together. They practiced only in household groups and at tournaments. For this reason, battle tactics were quite simple: a group of knights would charge the opposing army. The impact of an armored charge was enormous, but once committed to, it was hard to stop, and the knights might charge through the enemy and off the battlefield altogether. If ambushed from the flank, they were vulnerable because turning their horses in a mass charge was almost impossible. The victor was often the army that held the charge in reserve and attacked when their opponents were bogged down fighting foot soldiers or archers.

Foot soldiers
Along with knights and archers, armies needed foot soldiers to fight a battle. At first, foot soldiers were typically farmers forced into service, but during the long wars after 1300, career foot soldiers, well trained and armed, became more common.

A battle begins
The biggest army did not always win the battle. Cunning tactics often counted for more than strength in numbers. In this battle the blue army is charging the red, which seems vulnerable. But most of the red army was hidden in the woods and is now charging the flank of the blue.

Decoy camp *Tents offer a target for the blue army. They are protected by a fence, with crossbowmen to deflect and slow down the charge.*

Knights charge *Knights charge at the head of the blue army, hoping to smash the outnumbered reds.*

Bait *A group of knights on a hill, protected by spearmen, pretends to be the main red army.*

TOOLS OF WAR

Peasant foot soldiers would fight with any available weapons, even pitchforks. Professional men-at-arms chose weapons suited to their strengths. If they could afford it, a sword was best, but hammers and maces were good for stunning knights in plate armor.

Mace

War hammer

Buckler (top)
Shield (right)

Battle-ax

Flail

Dagger and sheath

Archer
Archers were an essential part of any army, but they had little protection if they were overrun.

Devilish crossbow
The crossbow was twice banned by the pope for being unsporting, but that did not stop its popularity in the later Middle Ages.

Rain of arrows *Archers kept behind in safety fire high in the air to break up the mass charge of the blues and cause confusion.*

Surprise attack *Once the blues are committed to the charge, the hidden red army strikes from the flank and is likely to defeat the enemy.*

Into the fray *Foot soldiers run behind the knights, ready for hand-to-hand fighting if the ranks of the red army are broken.*

Knights'
Last Stand

The tactics and technology of warfare gradually changed during the Middle Ages. Arrows fired from powerful bows made chain armor useless, so heavy plate armor that covered the whole body was developed. This armor was ruinously expensive. Eventually, several decisive battles were won by large numbers of skilled, lightly armed men on foot, using bows, long pikes, and later, guns to overcome the heavily armored knights. By the late 1400s, it was common for knights to send their horses back from battle and to fight on foot. Ultimately, the once invincible knights disappeared from the battlefield entirely.

New deal for knights
Social changes also contributed to the decline of knights. For many knights, it was better to pay a special tax to the king rather than risk their lives in battle. These taxes meant that the king could afford to pay for an army of skilled mercenaries while the knights could enjoy living well.

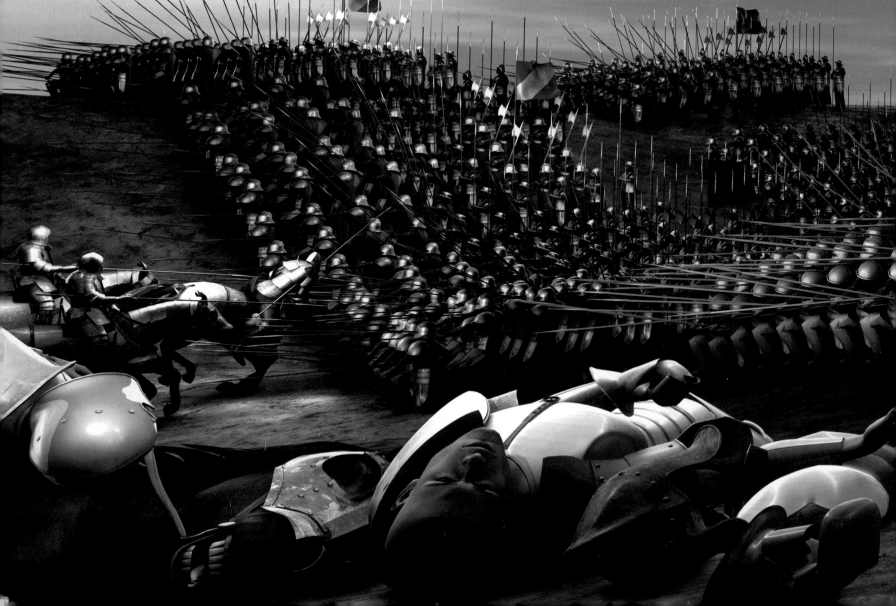

NEW WEAPONS OF WAR

By the late medieval period, even the strongest armor could be pierced by an arrow fired from a powerful crossbow, or a missile shot from a simple gun. As a result, a soldier with a few weeks' training could defeat a mighty knight.

Windlass crossbow, 1400s

Matchlock gun, late 1400s

Knights meet their match

This scene shows mounted knights confronted by skilled pikemen. The pikemen have gathered into tight formations with their long pikes protecting them. The knights are forced into narrow paths between the formations. With archers in range behind the pikemen, the knights are unhorsed and vulnerable.

The Need for
Castles

Castles were the fortified homes of lords in feudal societies. Initially, they were built to secure possession of conquered territory, but for centuries they served to maintain the power of the lords in times of peace as well as war. During the Middle Ages, alliances could change quickly, and the castle was a place of refuge for a lord and his supporters if he was attacked. A castle was also the base for the lord's own military campaigns. In times of peace, the castle was a center of administration and industry, and an intimidating symbol of power and wealth to the lord's many tenants.

An ideal castle

Given a free hand on a flat site, castle builders favored a symmetrical design and defense in depth, so that each part of the castle overlooked the area farther out. This way, archers could be stationed at several levels, each firing at the enemy outside. The result was the concentric castle, which provided massive strength but limited accommodation inside.

HOW A DRAWBRIDGE WORKS

A weak spot in a castle was the entrance, normally protected by a drawbridge. This could be raised on a winch by guards in a room above.

Slammed shut If needed, a heavy grilled gate called a portcullis could be dropped in an instant.

Access denied Below the drawbridge was a deep pit or a water-filled moat.

Outer ward *The outer ward housed the stables, workshops, and administrative buildings for the lord's tenants.*

Water barrier *A water-filled moat was often the first line of defense. A moat frustrated attackers' attempts to approach the walls or undermine them from below.*

Bird's-eye view
Archers used turrets to get a commanding view of the entire castle and the country beyond.

Drum tower
Massive cylindrical towers provided defense and useful rooms inside for accommodation.

Outer wall *The outer wall was about 30 feet (9 m) high and was overlooked by the towers and the wall of the inner courtyard.*

Inner ward *The inner ward was the central part of the castle, containing the hall, chamber, chapel, and kitchen for the lord.*

Preparing for trouble
Wooden hoardings allowed archers to fire at enemies at the base of the wall. They were kept in storage until needed.

Staircase
Access between floors was normally by spiral staircase. They were usually built to give advantage to a right-handed defender.

Castles
In Time

Castles are found throughout Europe, some parts of the Middle East, and Japan. Castle building reached its peak at different times in different places. The most impressive castles of the early Middle Ages were built in the Muslim world. In Japan, castles were built long after they were at their peak in Europe. Castles come in all shapes and sizes, depending on when they were built, their purpose, and local materials and building styles. The people that built these magnificent structures have now disappeared, but many castles remain as a reminder of a turbulent past.

Castle map
Castles were found in societies where local rulers held power, including most of Europe, and parts of the Middle East and Asia. This type of society, often called feudal, contrasted with great states, empires, and tribal societies, where castles were rare.

All shapes and sizes
Castles were built of wood, brick, or stone and could be grand or modest. What they all had in common were defensive structures to keep hostile forces out.

1 700s: Islamic castles
Qasr al-Hayr, Syria
The castles of the Muslim world include those built to protect trade routes and hundreds of castles built by the Moors in Spain and Portugal.

2 1000s: Motte and bailey
Knockgraffon Castle, Ireland
Timber castles spread across Europe during the 1000s and 1100s. Often these took the form of a motte (an earthen mount) and bailey (a fortified enclosure).

3 1100s: Stone keeps
Rochester Castle, England
Beginning with the kings, lords began to replace their timber castles with stone keeps, often with tall and massive towers that reflected their status.

4 1100s–1200s: Crusader castles
Krak des Chevaliers, Syria
Constant threats forced the crusaders to build ever-stronger fortresses. By 1200 only the greatest lords could afford to build them, and most were funded by holy orders of knights.

AD 500
600
700
800
900
1000
1100
1200

8
1500s–early 1600s: Japanese castles
Himeji Castle, Japan
While in Europe castles were in
decline, the shoguns (nobles) of
Japan seized power and built their
own massive fortified houses to
guard against their enemies.

9
1800s: Fantasy castles
Neuschwanstein Castle, Germany
Historic novels and fantasies made
castle style popular in the 1800s.
Many wealthy rulers and industrial
barons chose to rebuild old castles
or create completely new ones.

5
1150–1250: Germanic castles
Heidenreichstein Castle, Austria
In Germany and eastern Europe, fragmented
kingdoms were common, and so castles
remained essential for protection long after
the need was reduced elsewhere in Europe.

1900

1800

1700

1600

1400

1300

1500

7
1500s: Palatial castles
Château d'Azay-le-Rideau, France
When society became more stable
and the need for physical protection
decreased, homes for the nobility became
less like fortresses and more like palaces.
But castle style survived as part of the
design of great houses, since a nobleman
still needed battlements and turrets to
demonstrate his status.

6
1250s: Concentric castles
Beaumaris Castle, Wales
After conquering Wales, the
English king Edward I built
massive castles to control the
country. Some were among
the strongest and most
expensive ever built.

Castle
Construction

Building a castle was a huge job. Dozens of stonemasons were required, together with carpenters, blacksmiths, and laborers—as many as 500, or even more for urgent projects—all under the charge of a master mason. Normally it took about 10 years to build a castle, longer if money ran out, which it often did. In most of Europe, work had to stop over winter because the frost damaged the mortar and stopped it from setting. While they waited for spring, the masons cut stones in work sheds, ready for the next year. The rest of the workforce returned home.

Busy building

In many ways, the castle building site was not all that different from its modern equivalent. Perhaps the biggest difference was that in the Middle Ages, everything was done through muscle power alone.

Treadmill crane *Heavy blocks were lifted by a man-powered treadmill crane.*

Masons *With hammers and chisels, masons shaped and smoothed roughly cut blocks to fit neatly in place, using lead and thin timber templates to match the shapes.*

Making mortar *Medieval mortar was made from burned lime, which was soaked in pits, then mixed with sand.*

Master mason *The master mason was architect, engineer, and site manager. He learned his craft by working for years under other masons.*

Rubble *Medieval buildings were built with skins of fine stone, between which rubble and mortar were poured to form a solid wall.*

Blacksmiths *Ironworkers were needed to make hinges, nails, and other fittings, and would constantly forge and sharpen tools for the masons.*

BUILDING TOOLS

The tools of the craftsmen have changed very little, right up to today, and include hammers, chisels, drills (brace and bit), and frame saws. Indeed, the same tools were used in Roman times.

Mason's ax

Hammer

Compass

Mason's mallet

Stone chisels

Frame saw

Carpenter's brace

Carpenter's ax

Mason's marks

Masons were usually paid for the number of finished blocks they produced. In order to keep track of who was owed what, each mason carved his own personal symbol into his stones.

The Castle
Besieged

Conquering castles was a big part of medieval warfare. No invading army could control an area without controlling the castles there. They could not ignore them and march past, for fear of being attacked from behind later. There were two basic ways for an army to take a castle. The first was to get inside and then overpower the occupants. Getting inside meant either smashing their way in or scaling over the walls. The second was to surround the castle and starve the occupants into submission. This could take months.

Scorched earth *When the castle occupants knew the enemy was coming, they quickly burned their houses and crops, and cleared away anything that could help the besiegers, including food stores and timber.*

Starting the siege

Here the attacking army is mounting an assault using archers, siege engines, and a siege tower. If this initial attack fails, and if the defenders do not surrender, it could be the start of a long siege.

Smashing *Three or four blows in the same place from a trebuchet missile were enough to demolish the top of a wall. The shock of the blows alone might seriously demoralize the defenders.*

Shelter *Wood and wickerwork screens allowed the attacking archers to get close to the walls of the castle.*

Mangonel *The mangonel was not as accurate or powerful as a trebuchet, but it was easy to build and maneuver.*

BATTLE MACHINES

As is the case today, some of the most sophisticated technology of the Middle Ages was developed for waging war.

Mangonel
These catapults were powered by the tension of twisted ropes of hair or sinew. They could hurl a missile up to 650 feet (200 m).

Siege tower
The greatest siege towers were as high as a 10-story building and could carry dozens of archers and multiple catapults.

Over the top *No matter how destructive the attack with siege engines, the only way of capturing a castle was an assault through the gate or over the battlements. Siege towers loaded with troops were used to breach the walls.*

Boarded up *Wooden hoardings ensured that the bases of the walls were not safe places for attackers, but they were vulnerable to fire arrows and siege engines.*

TREBUCHET

The largest missiles were thrown by trebuchets, which used counterweights and long hinged beams with slings. Experiments show that they could throw stones weighing 300 pounds (135 kg) up to 400 yards (365 m). However, the machines needed constant attention to keep them from falling apart.

1 The trebuchet is ready.

2 The trebuchet is triggered and the counterweight drops.

3 The missile is released from the sling.

4 The mechanism comes to rest.

Attack and

Defense

During the Middle Ages, castle design constantly evolved, bringing steady improvements in castle security. But for every defensive advance came a new ingenious tactic or clever piece of technology to overcome it. Because of this, siege battles were often closely matched and ferociously fought. When they occurred, each side used every technique to overcome the other, such as missiles, archery, battering rams, fire, tunneling, and even cutting through walls using pickaxes. Even the strongest castle could be seized without any direct force. The garrison could be bribed to surrender, or the castle inhabitants tricked into thinking their allies had abandoned them.

Break and enter

The gatehouse was designed to allow the passage of carts and wagons, so it was an obvious place for an attacking army to try to force entry. However, castle designers and defenders had a few tricks for keeping them out.

SIEGE MISSILES

Stones were the most common siege missiles, but a wide range of objects were thrown back and forth, including burning pots to start fires, boiling-hot liquids, and dead animals to spread disease and demoralize the defenders.

Boulder bombs
Rounded stones flew the farthest and straightest.

On the boil
Pots of boiling oil or water were best tipped on attackers from above.

Firepots
These flaming clay pots broke apart on impact, spreading fire.

Dead on arrival
Animal corpses were used as a form of germ warfare.

Deadly downpour
Boiling water, or oil if available, was poured from above through holes in the battlements called machicolations.

Given the shove
Attacks using ladders were among the most dangerous (but most direct) ways of capturing a castle. Defenders used long poles to push them away.

Portcullis *This heavy wood and iron grille was the last line of defense.*

Tunneling tactics *Miners had to be wary of countermining tunneling by the castle soldiers. If the tunnels intersected, there might be a fierce battle underground.*

Undermined *If a castle was not built on rock, miners dug tunnels under the foundations. These were used for surprise attacks, or the props were set on fire to bring down the walls above.*

The Castle at
Peace

Many castles were never put to the test by a siege, and all were normally places of peaceful activity. Because they were homes to royals and nobles, all activities enjoyed by the upper classes took place inside and around the castle, from feasting to embroidery, from military training to courtship. As centers of power, castles were the place for government, politics, and conspiracies. They were also where the lord's farmlands were administered and rents collected, and where workshops for the estate's carpenters and metalworkers were located. Behind the strong walls, gold and important documents were kept.

Inside and out
Fortresses from the outside, castles were designed inside to be comfortable and impressive homes for the leaders of the land, and functional workplaces for lots of busy people.

Chapel
Daily religious services were a vital part of life, and chapels were provided for all to attend. The noble family had a private chapel for their worship.

Keeping guard *Even in times of peace, entrance to the castle was strictly controlled. Guarding against thieves was the main concern.*

Place to go *Toilets were built into the thickness of the wall and discharged into cesspits or outside at the base of the wall.*

Sleeping out
When the lord was resident, some of the castle's occupants needed lodging outside, in cottages or inns in the villages beside the castle.

Workshops
Workshops, generally in the outer ward, housed workers who made furniture, barrels, metalwork, and everything else needed by the inhabitants of the castle.

Kitchen
A castle with its lord and family in residence might need to accommodate 200 to 300 people, and the amount of food required was huge. Kitchens were correspondingly large.

Garrison *The garrison was where the soldiers slept and kept their equipment. As few as a dozen soldiers were kept in times of peace to save on their wages.*

Lord's quarters
The lord and his family occupied a small suite of private rooms isolated from the rest of the castle by guarded doors and staircases.

Well *A constant supply of fresh water was vital and was normally provided by wells cut as much as 300 feet (90 m) into the underlying rock.*

Rough justice
Punishment was immediate: for serious crimes, death; for minor crimes, the pillory, where people were pelted with dung or rotten vegetables.

COURTLY LOVE

Marriage was an important way for noble families to build alliances and maintain their power. Courtship was a formal affair, with chaperones and matchmakers. Poets, painters, and singers idealized the concept of romantic love, but in reality, marriages were arranged for the best political and financial outcome. Women lost most of their rights once they were married. The poor, however, with little to lose, had much greater freedom to marry whom they wished.

Castle People
Who's Who

Only a small group of people lived in the castle year-round, including the porter, or gatekeeper, and a few soldiers. They were looked after by the constable, who might live elsewhere, but had rooms in the castle. The steward had his office in the castle, but his duties took him off around the estate. When the lord was there, the castle was filled with his household of servants, most of whom traveled around with the family. Up to two or three hundred people needed to find rooms in the castle or in the neighboring villages and towns.

Castle cast

Illustrated here are some of the officials, servants, and men at arms who looked after the lord and his family, and were often called "the household" or the "lord's familiars."

Noble family *The family and the children were the center of noble life. Boys inherited the lands, and girls eventually married into the families of important allies.*

Steward *The steward looked after the estates and made sure that everything ran smoothly in the household.*

Gong farmer *The gong farmer had one of the worst jobs in the castle—cleaning out cesspits and latrines.*

Cook *The cook—usually a man—was in charge of as many as 20 people in the kitchen.*

Lady-in-waiting *The lady's maid ensured that the lady had clean clothes, looked after her hair and appearance, and was a constant companion to her.*

Priest *All castles had a priest or chaplain, who performed daily masses in the castle chapel for the whole household.*

Constable *The constable controlled the defenses of the castle. He generally had rooms in the gatehouse, to watch those who came and went.*

Prisoner *Castles sometimes had a dungeon for locking up common criminals, but many prisoners were important people, even kings, who were held for ransom and were usually treated well.*

Soldier *The household normally included 10 to 20 trained soldiers, some of whom stayed there all year, while some traveled with the lord on his journeys.*

Archer *Most castles included a few trained archers in their garrisons. In times of war, many more were summoned from their farms in the nearby countryside.*

Barber *The barber cut the household's hair, as barbers do now, but he also acted as the doctor, with a little knowledge of folk medicine and primitive surgery.*

Houndsman *The houndsman looked after the hunting dogs.*

Armorer *The armorer was a skilled metalworker who made weapons and armor. For rough ironwork the castle relied on blacksmiths.*

Groom *A household had 10 or more grooms. They fed, groomed, and looked after the horses.*

Working the Castle Land

Most castles now stand in towns, surrounded by houses, or are empty ruins on hills or in woods. But in the Middle Ages, they were the center of great estates, with farms to provide grain and fruit for the household, and villages where peasants lived. Most people in the Middle Ages worked on the land, and their lives revolved around the changing seasons. Peasants were tenants of the castle lord. They cut the wood, plowed the fields, and did other duties for the lord, such as serving as soldiers or building barns and stables for him. The lord's wealth came almost exclusively from the rents these peasants paid and from the sale of surplus food or wool the peasants had produced.

Winter *Winter is the season for digging ditches, cutting wood, spreading manure on the fields, making and repairing tools, and building fences. Seeds lie dormant in the ground, waiting for spring.*

Spring *Spring is a time for plowing and sowing seed for harvest in the fall, and for taking care of newborn lambs.*

Summer labor
In 1420 a French duke commissioned a series of 12 paintings, one for each month, to show the changing seasons. "July" shows sheepshearing and hay reaping in the shadow of a great castle.

Cycle of the seasons
In northern Europe, agriculture revolved around the three-field system. In each year, two fields were sown and harvested while one was left fallow to recover its nutrients. It would then be ready for the following year.

Field three Fallow field (used for field sports)

Field two Seeds dormant in soil

Field one Spreading manure

Maypole dance The coming of spring was cause for celebration.

On guard Shepherds kept the flock safe from foxes and thieves.

Field three Fallow field plowed to bury weeds, which act as a fertilizer

Field two Wheat crop is growing

Field one Field ploughed and sown for fall harvest

Summer In summer the wheat crop is harvested, the sheep are shorn of their wool, and grass is cut for hay to feed the cattle over winter.

Shearing Wool was a valuable commodity and made many lords rich.

Field three Fallow field

Harvest Peasants used sharp iron sickles to harvest crops.

Field one Crops of oats or barley alternated with rows of beans and peas growing

Field two Wheat harvested

Fall Fall is a busy season. Oats and barley are harvested, some livestock are taken to market or slaughtered, pigs are let loose to fatten on acorns, honey and apples are harvested, and grapes are pressed to make wine.

Next year's vintage Grapes were crushed by foot in big barrels.

Field three Field ploughed and sown for next summer's wheat harvest

Field two New fallow field

Field one Harvest of oats or barley, beans, and peas

Castle Leisure

While there was always work to be done in and around the castle, there was time for leisure as well. Every Sunday was a day of rest, and there were also many saint's days and local festivals to enjoy. Noblewomen enjoyed activities such as embroidery, tapestry, and listening to music, while men hunted or played games of chess. Gardens were a feature of many castles and were admired for their herbs and flowers. Team sports included a riotous type of football with dozens or even hundreds of players and hardly any rules.

Read all about it
In early medieval times, only priests and clerks learned to read. But by 1400, a change occurred as literacy became more widespread. This photo shows a hand-drawn French "book of hours" (prayer book) from the late 1400s. At this time, the growing demand for books inspired the invention of the printing press.

Chess in a formal garden
Board games, such as draughts and chess, were extremely popular. Even the names of the pieces—kings, bishops, and knights—were named for people of the Middle Ages.

Sky hunters *Falcons and other birds of prey kill on the wing with their sharp talons. Trained hunting birds got to eat the head and neck of the prey—the rest was food for the table.*

The "sport of kings"
The upper classes enjoyed hunting deer and boars with dogs, and training birds of prey to attack pigeons and other birds. Falconry was known as the "sport of kings" because it was an expensive pastime.

Birds of privilege *In some places, only kings, princes, and dukes could own falcons. Knights and commoners were restricted to hunting with hawks and kestrels.*

The hunted *Pigeons, ducks, pheasants, and herons were all targets. Rabbits and hares could also fall prey to the fast strike of a falcon or hawk.*

COCKFIGHTING

One of the most popular forms of entertainment among the lower classes was watching and betting on fights between animals. Fights between cockerels, between dogs, and between dogs and bears were particularly popular.

Born to fight *Fighting cockerels were specially bred for stamina and strength.*

Tough glove *Thick leather gloves protected the falconer's hand from the bird's sharp talons.*

Spurs *Often, small blades were fastened to the cockerels' legs. This ensured that the cockfight was a fight to the death.*

Entertainment and
Banquets

A lord who provided food for his household, guests, tenants, and travelers was thought to be noble, and if the banquet was huge, so too was the honor. The greatest feasts had hundreds of guests with multiple courses, mostly of meat, bread, and sweets. Some banquets were for special guests; others were held at regular intervals for farm tenants and other locals. In fact, every night when the lord was at home, the household, visitors, and passersby might expect to dine together in the castle hall. By these means, the lord cemented together the loyalty of his followers, without which his power diminished.

Hall hierarchy

Seating in the hall was formal. The lord and noble guests sat at the high table, raised at the farthest end of the hall from the kitchen. The rest sat on benches beside trestle tables arranged down the hall, with the poorest farthest from the high table.

Jester *As well as music, entertainment was provided by jesters, who danced, made riddles, sang songs, and told jokes, most of which were coarse.*

Trenchers *Plates were reserved for nobles. Most people ate off a piece of stale bread called a trencher.*

MAKING MUSIC

M usic was played at most ceremonies. Large banquets in the hall were entertained with rhythmic dance music and marches played on loud brass trumpets and woodwind instruments, accompanied by fiddle or reeded pipes. Intimate gatherings in the chamber would hear love songs on the lute or flutes.

Trumpet

Lute

Recorder

Rebec

Shawm

Musicians *Trumpeters in the gallery, and a lute and a harp player in the hall, accompany the jester's dance.*

Exotic foods *This special dish—a dolphin—is brought up for the lord's inspection before being distributed to the guests. Providing such exotic food was good for the lord's prestige.*

Castles
In Decline

The introduction of gunpowder and cannons complicated the design of castles but did not immediately cause their end. Early cannons did not work well and were as much use in defending castles as attacking them. Many castles proved hard to capture with artillery, even as late as the 1600s. However, building castles that could withstand cannon fire was expensive, and eventually even the richest nobles could not afford them. Meanwhile, Europe gradually became a more stable place and the need to live behind strong walls diminished. Many castles fell into ruin, their stones carried away to make other buildings.

Charcoal
2 parts

Sulfur
3 parts

Saltpeter
15 parts

An explosive mix
Gunpowder is a mix of saltpeter (a mineral sourced from manure and stale urine), charcoal (partially burned wood), and sulfur (a mineral that was mined). Gunpowder was invented in China more than a thousand years ago. Europeans learned how to make it in the 1200s—the knowledge was passed along the Silk Road by traders and merchants.

Bringing down the house
Early cannons were most effective when fired at point-blank range. Gunners made an easy target for castle defenders and were often killed. They were paid a lot of money to take such risks and used every protection they could devise.

CANNONS IN ACTION

Early cannons were commonly made of iron tubes bound together by rings. Gunpowder releases its energy fairly slowly when burning, but even so, the barrels of early guns often burst when fired. Scotland's King James II was killed by an exploding cannon while laying siege to an English castle in 1460.

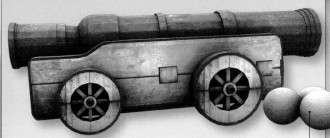

Wadding
Plug
Gunpowder
Chamber
Cannonballs Stone cannonballs were preferred over iron ones because they were less likely to burst the barrel.

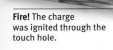

Fire! The charge was ignited through the touch hole.

This illustration shows a typical cannon from about 1500. Such cannons were used on land as well as mounted on the decks of ships.

Deal Castle
Deal Castle is not really a castle. It is a military fort built on the orders of King Henry VIII to protect the south coast of England. It shows how architects responded to the challenge of artillery. Its low, rounded gun platforms deflected missiles and presented a small target to attacking guns.

Living like a lord
Castles were never comfortable places to live. When the protection they offered was no longer needed, wealthy nobles were quick to build grand houses, with all the latest luxuries, outside the castle walls.

AD 1500

Locator map This map of Europe shows you exactly where the featured castle is located. Look for the red dot on each map.

North Sea

ENGLAND

London

Paris

Mont-Saint-Michel

Loire

Atlantic Ocean

FRANCE

Bordeaux

Marseille

SPAIN

MONT-SAINT-MICHEL: THE FACTS

WHEN IT WAS BUILT: Abbey established 708, main fortifications constructed 1420s

WHERE IT WAS BUILT: Normandy, France

WHO BUILT IT: Order of Saint Benedict

MATERIALS: Granite

SIZE: 10 acres (4 ha)

Fast facts Fast facts at your fingertips give you essential information on each castle being explored.

AD 1400

AD 1300

AD 1200

AD 1100

Time bar This time bar shows when the castle was constructed. The bar covers the period from AD 1000 to AD 1500.

AD 1000

Becoming a
Knight

When a boy who was to become a knight reached the age of seven, he was sent away from his family to be a page in the castle of a lord, usually a friend of his father's or an uncle. At the age of about fourteen, he was apprenticed to a knight and became a squire. Then followed another five to seven years of training before he was ready to become a knight. Because a knight's horses, armor, and servants cost so much money, only boys from the richest families could become knights.

① School *The young page was given a basic education by the castle chaplain. This included some history, geography, religion, and a little reading and writing—at least enough to sign his name and read the accounts prepared by his steward when he became a knight.*

② Table manners *The page was taught good manners and served the lord at table. He might be beaten if he did not behave correctly.*

③ Master and servant *When the page became a squire, he was taught about armor and helped his master to dress. He was also expected to follow his master to battle.*

④ Learning to fight *Because armor and weapons were so heavy, learning to fight involved lots of physical training. Squires staged mock fights and battles using wooden swords and shields.*

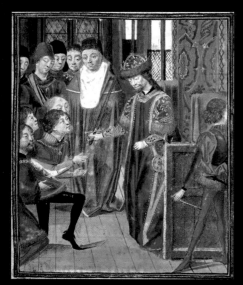

The big day
This French illustration from the 1400s shows two squires being dubbed by their king. Courtiers have gathered to observe this important occasion.

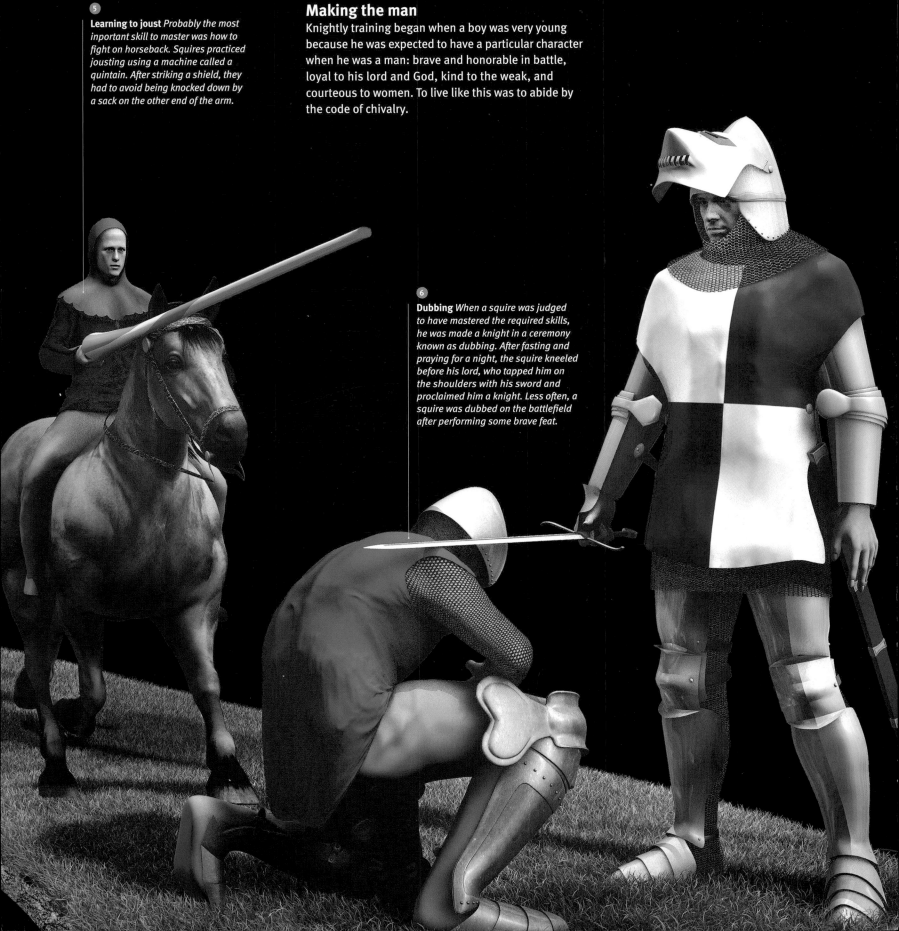

5 **Learning to joust** *Probably the most inportant skill to master was how to fight on horseback. Squires practiced jousting using a machine called a quintain. After striking a shield, they had to avoid being knocked down by a sack on the other end of the arm.*

Making the man

Knightly training began when a boy was very young because he was expected to have a particular character when he was a man: brave and honorable in battle, loyal to his lord and God, kind to the weak, and courteous to women. To live like this was to abide by the code of chivalry.

6 **Dubbing** *When a squire was judged to have mastered the required skills, he was made a knight in a ceremony known as dubbing. After fasting and praying for a night, the squire kneeled before his lord, who tapped him on the shoulders with his sword and proclaimed him a knight. Less often, a squire was dubbed on the battlefield after performing some brave feat.*

A Knight's Armor and

Weapons

The knight in battle always wore armor, which was made of hammered steel and weighed as much as 55 pounds (25 kg). Early armor was made from interlocking rings and was called chain mail. It was flexible but it could be pierced by arrows. From the 1200s onward, plates of steel, held together with buckles and straps, were gradually added for extra protection. By the end of the 1400s armor was worn over all the body. This was called plate armor, and the best (decorated in gold and silver) cost as much as a soldier might earn in 10 years. A knight's normal weapons were the lance, the sword or ax, and sometimes blades on long poles, called pikes, with hooks to catch on the straps of his enemy's armor.

Battle ready

This knight is wearing full plate armor. Beneath the armor he wears an arming doublet—a jacket of chain mail, padded cloth, and leather. The plates of armor were fitted to the arming doublet, which prevented the armor from pinching his body.

CHAIN MAIL

Making chain mail was an intricate and labor-intensive job. As many as 30,000 separate rings needed to be made and linked together to make just one coat of chain mail.

Coil
First heavy wire was wrapped around a rod.

Snipped
The coil was cut with hand snips.

Into the die
The loops were forced through a tapered die to make the ends overlap.

Completed circle
The ends were beaten flat, punctured, and closed with a tiny rivet when in place.

Rings of confidence
The rings of chain mail can be linked in a variety of different patterns, but in medieval Europe the 1-into-4 pattern (where each ring is linked with four others) was dominant.

Mail gusset

Helmet

Mail gorget

Spaulders

Couter

Lance rest

Cannon of the vambrace

Gauntlet

Breastplate

Linen undershirt

Fauld of five lames

Armor 1100s
The knight in the 1100s wore a long coat of chain mail, which came down to his knees. He normally wore a cloth coat (called a "surcoat") over the armor, especially in hot weather.

Armor 1300s
In the 1300s the knight wore plate armor over many parts of his body. Any exposed areas, such as his neck and the back of his legs, were protected by chain mail.

Leather shoe

Hose

Tasset

Mail skirt

Cuisse

Poleyn

Greave

Sabaton

Crossguard

Fuller

Sword
The sword was the knight's favored weapon in close combat. It was also a prized possession and a symbol of his status. A knight wore his sword hung from his waist even when not in armor. The sword illustrated here is a two-handed longsword.

The Mounted
Knight

A knight on horseback was by far the most powerful and feared soldier of the middle ages. A knight's warhorse had to be strong, brave, and nimble as well. In battle the knight was most effective when charging, but with his heavy armor, he was very vulnerable if he was thrown off his horse, or if his enemies got under the horse and stabbed it. To prevent this, horses were trained to keep trampling and twisting about when they were surrounded by footsoldiers. Along with his armor and his sword, his warhorse was a knight's most valuable possession. A good warhorse could cost 20 times as much as a regular horse, and many knights had more than one.

Riding to war

When traveling, the knight's entourage included his warhorses, a packhorse to carry his armor and belongings, and a palfrey or riding horse, on which he rode. His page led the warhorses.

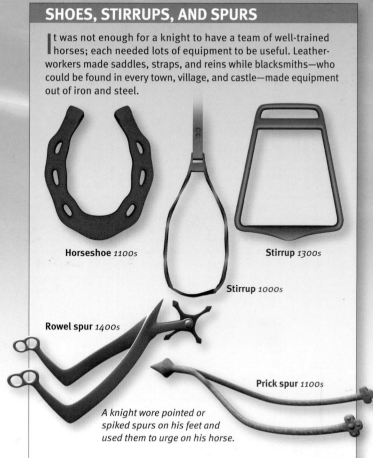

SHOES, STIRRUPS, AND SPURS

It was not enough for a knight to have a team of well-trained horses; each needed lots of equipment to be useful. Leatherworkers made saddles, straps, and reins while blacksmiths—who could be found in every town, village, and castle—made equipment out of iron and steel.

Horseshoe *1100s*

Stirrup *1300s*

Stirrup *1000s*

Rowel spur *1400s*

Prick spur *1100s*

A knight wore pointed or spiked spurs on his feet and used them to urge on his horse.

Chaffron *The most important piece of horse armor was the chaffron, which protected the horse's face.*

Here comes the cavalry

Here the knight is prepared for battle as he would be in hostile territory, but his shield and weapons are still being carried by his page. Steel armor for horses became common from the 1400s onward.

Crinet *The crinet was made of overlapping plates and protected the horse's neck.*

Safe and secure
The raised pommel (front) and cantle (rear) gave the knight added security in battle.

Belt up *The girth was a wide strap that went around the horse's chest.*

War saddle
War saddles had to be attached very securely to ensure they did not shift with the weight of a fully armored knight.

Flanchards *The flanchards protected the sides of the horse, below the saddle.*

Crupper *The crupper protected the horse's rump.*

Peytral *The horse's chest was armored with the peytral.*

Jousting
Practice for War

Knights constantly practiced fighting on foot and on horseback in preparation for actual war. From the 1100s onward this training became a hugely popular form of entertainment—knights gathered from far and wide to see who was the most skilled fighter of all. The most exciting event was jousting, when two knights charged at each other on horseback holding lances. Knights could be killed jousting, but it was worth the risk to be thought a brave and skilled knight. For knights with little money or from unimportant families, jousting was a way to become rich and famous.

HERALDRY

Because every knight looked the same in armor, they started painting colored patterns and pictures on their shields so they could be recognized in battle. This was known as heraldry and it is something from the middle ages that we see every day in the modern world.

Heraldic charges
The patterns and pictures of heraldry are known as charges. Below are eight charges, but there are hundreds more.

Chief

Pale

Bend

Chevron

Cross

Wavy

Lion rampant

Swan passant

When two important families were joined in marriage they combined their arms by dividing the shield. This was called quartering.

Husband's arms

Wife's arms

Crashing knights

Here two knights are jousting in front of an audience in a grandstand. They ride on opposite sides of a barrier to keep them in line. The knight in red will score points for having broken his lance against his opponent and for knocking the blue knight off his horse.

Battle-ax battle

This French illustration from the 1400s shows two knights about to fight with blunted battle-axes in front of an audience of nobles. The two men on either side are marshals who made sure that the knights obeyed the rules.

The Tower of London, England

Castle to Kings

In 1066, the Norman French conquered England. The Norman king, William the Conqueror, chose London as his capital. To control the city, he decided to build a great tower in the corner of the old Roman walls. This became known as the White Tower, for the color of its stone. Over the next three centuries, a huge castle complex, called the Tower of London, was constructed around the White Tower, protected by walls and a moat. Originally, this castle was the center of royal power and a refuge for the royal family in times of disorder. Later, it became a feared prison for enemies of the state and was a storehouse for weapons and treasure.

Capital castle

This is a bird's-eye view of the Tower of London in about 1600. At this time, the castle complex included the royal apartments, a church and burial ground, the royal mint, a storage place for gunpowder, and the royal arsenal—a mass of storerooms and workshops where cannons were made.

Losing your head

Execution by beheading was normally reserved for nobles convicted of treason. Beheadings usually took place at Tower Hill, just outside the walls of the castle. Royals were luckier—they were executed in the privacy of the castle grounds.

THE TOWER TODAY

The Tower of London is still a royal fortress, with a garrison and an arsenal. Thousands of people visit each year to see one of the most historic spots in England.

Tower treasures The Crown Jewels and other treasures, including royal armor, are kept inside the Tower, in a strongroom built for the purpose.

Beefeaters A garrison of Yeoman Warders (popularly known as "Beefeaters") guard the Tower and guide visitors. They are all retired soldiers.

AD 1500

AD 1400

AD 1300

AD 1200

AD 1100

AD 1000

C. 1100: WHITE TOWER BUILT

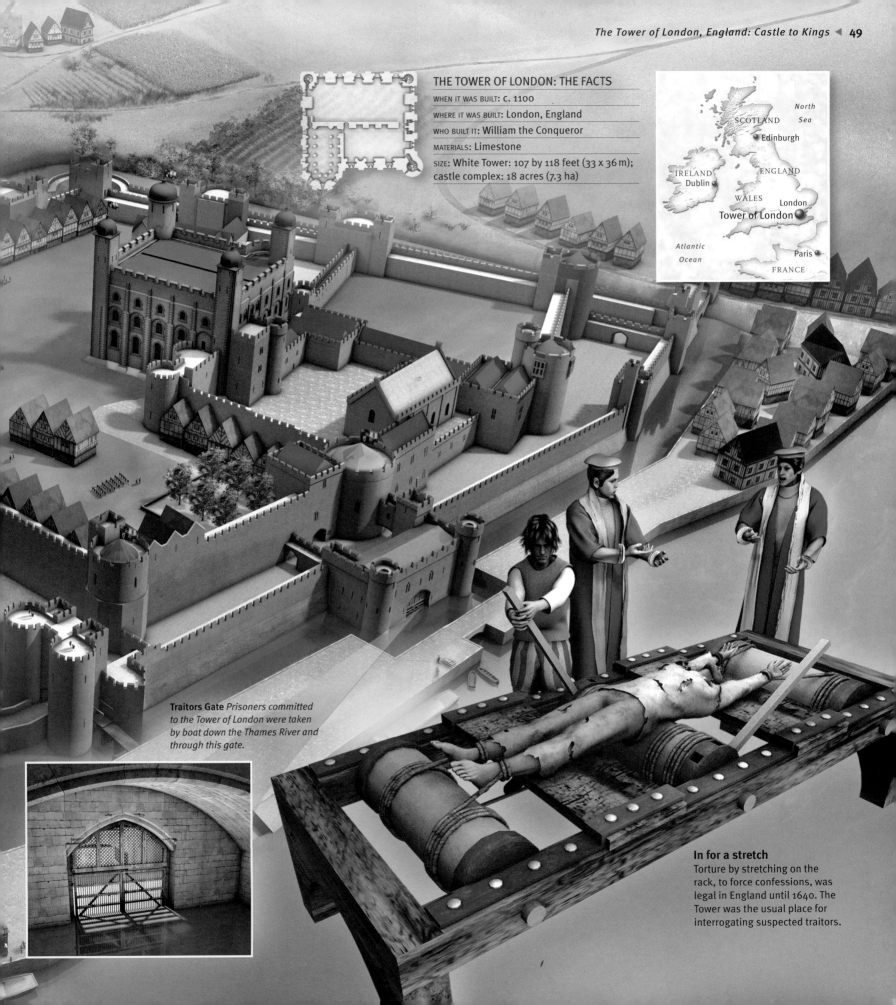

THE TOWER OF LONDON: THE FACTS

WHEN IT WAS BUILT: C. 1100

WHERE IT WAS BUILT: London, England

WHO BUILT IT: William the Conqueror

MATERIALS: Limestone

SIZE: White Tower: 107 by 118 feet (33 x 36 m); castle complex: 18 acres (7.3 ha)

Traitors Gate *Prisoners committed to the Tower of London were taken by boat down the Thames River and through this gate.*

In for a stretch
Torture by stretching on the rack, to force confessions, was legal in England until 1640. The Tower was the usual place for interrogating suspected traitors.

AD 1500

AD 1400

AD 1300

AD 1250

CRUSADER RECONSTRUCTION

AD 1150

AD 1100

AD 1031: FORTRESS BUILT

AD 1000

Krak des Chevaliers, Syria
Knight's Rock

The crusader castle of Krak des Chevaliers ("fortress of the knights") is thought by many to be the finest castle in the world. It stands above a strategic pass through the mountains that once lay on the border of the crusader kingdoms. Originally a small Arab fortress, it was taken over by the Knights Hospitallers in 1142, who rebuilt it on a vast scale. It was so strong that even the great general Saladin, who won Jerusalem from the crusaders, decided not to attack it. In 1271, when most of the crusader kingdoms had fallen, the knights received a letter by carrier pigeon apparently from their commander in Tripoli, ordering them to surrender. The letter was a forgery and so the great castle was lost through trickery.

Black Sea
Istanbul
TURKEY
CYPRUS
Mediterranean Sea
Krak
LEBANON
ISRAEL
Jerusalem
EGYPT   Cairo

KRAK DES CHEVALIERS: THE FACTS

WHEN IT WAS BUILT: 1031 (original fortress), c. 1150–1250 (crusader reconstruction)

WHERE IT WAS BUILT: Near Homs, Syria

WHO BUILT IT: Emir of Aleppo (original fortress), Knights Hospitallers (crusader reconstruction)

MATERIALS: Basalt and limestone

SIZE: 650 by 460 feet (200 x 140 m); 7.5 acres (3 ha)

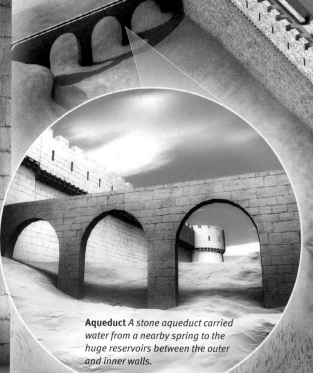

Aqueduct *A stone aqueduct carried water from a nearby spring to the huge reservoirs between the outer and inner walls.*

Knights Hospitallers
The Knights Hospitallers were a religious order of knights who were sworn to care for and defend pilgrims to the Holy Land.

View from above

The inner castle was used for ceremonies and official business and included a fine stone chapel. Beneath the inner castle and behind the outer walls were rooms for knights and visitors, storerooms, and stables.

Windmill *A windmill was built to grind fresh flour for the garrison even during a long siege.*

Enter here *There was only one way into the heart of the castle— a narrow, twisting passageway protected at every point by arrow slits and murder holes.*

Unbreakable *The wall of the inner ward, which was exposed to higher ground where enemy catapults could be placed, was 100 feet (30 m) high and 80 feet (25 m) thick.*

CASTLE REFUGE

Although the normal garrison at the castle was no more than a few dozen knights, Krak des Chevaliers was designed to accommodate up to two thousand soldiers and refugees for a year or more. To do this there were vast vaulted storerooms for food, deep reservoirs of water, and stables for more than five hundred horses.

Castel del Monte, Italy
Riddle in Stone

On a hilltop in a remote and quiet corner of southern Italy stands one of the world's most extraordinary and mysterious castles. It was built in about 1240 by Frederick II, the Holy Roman Emperor, who was one of the most powerful and learned men of his times. He could speak seven languages and was steeped in the wisdom of the Western, Arab, and classical Greek and Roman worlds. Castel del Monte was an expression in stone of his knowledge and philosophy. It was designed in harmony with many geometric and mathematical principles as well as the movement of the Sun through the year. A lot of the symbolism built into the castle was considered secret knowledge, and no records survive to tell us what it all might mean. But the castle remains, daring us to unravel its mysteries.

(left margin timeline)
AD 1500
AD 1400
AD 1300
C. 1240: CASTEL DEL MONTE BUILT
AD 1200
AD 1100
AD 1000

CASTEL DEL MONTE: THE FACTS
WHEN IT WAS BUILT: C. 1240

WHERE IT WAS BUILT: Apulia, Italy

WHO BUILT IT: Frederick II, Holy Roman Emperor

MATERIALS: Limestone and marble

SIZE: 180 feet (55 m) across

In perfect harmony
The castle's plan is based around the octagon. This shape represents a midpoint between the square (the Earth) and the circle (the celestial sphere). Using Roman feet, all elements of the plan and elevation are multiples of 12, long considered to be one of the luckiest numbers.

AN EXERCISE IN GEOMETRY

In Frederick's time, the rediscovery of Arab and Greek philosophy had a great influence on architecture, mathematics, and music. Numbers and geometry were thought to reflect both the real and heavenly worlds. A building was better—more holy, powerful, and beautiful—if its design was based around certain numbers and shapes.

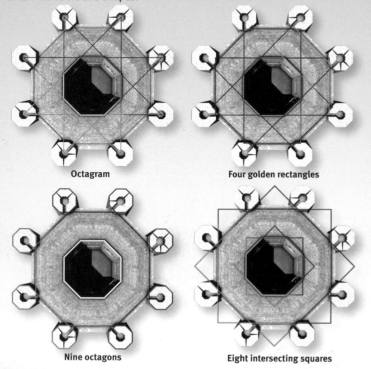

Octagram

Four golden rectangles

Nine octagons

Eight intersecting squares

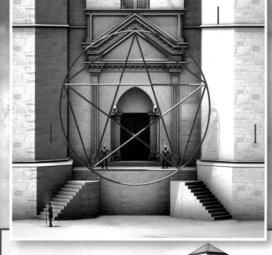

Pentagram door
The doorway is designed around the proportions and angles of a pentagram. This five-pointed star has been an important symbol since the time of ancient Egypt.

Put to use
Castel del Monte did have a practical application. Frederick II used it as a hunting lodge. Later it was used as a prison.

Frederick II
As well as being Holy Roman Emperor, Frederick II was king of Sicily, southern Italy, and parts of Germany.

AD 1500

AD 1400

AD 1300

AD 1271: CONSTRUCTION COMPLETED

AD 1200

AD 1100

AD 1000

Caerphilly, Wales
Shielded by Water

Wales is often called "the land of castles." Centuries of struggle for control of this corner of Britain have left a legacy of hundreds of castles, some of which represent the pinnacle of castle design. In 1266 Gilbert de Clare, one of the greatest nobles in England, seized territory from Llewelyn the Last, "Last" because he was the last prince of an independent Wales. Gilbert began to build a vast new castle at Caerphilly to control his estates. Llewelyn attacked but was driven off, and the castle was completed soon after. Caerphilly soon lost its importance as a fortress, though it remained an administrative center, and was attacked during the civil wars of the 1320s and 1640s.

THE CONQUEST OF WALES

Not long after the Normans conquered England in 1066, they began to conquer the territory of the Welsh. To secure these lands, the Norman lords built many castles (which are marked in purple below). Caerphilly (in red) is the greatest of these castles. Later, the native Welsh of the north fought back. In response, King Edward I of England launched two invasions, building his own castles as he went and rebuilding Welsh castles to ensure the conquest (the yellow castles on the map). By 1300 all of Wales was captured and occupied by the Norman English.

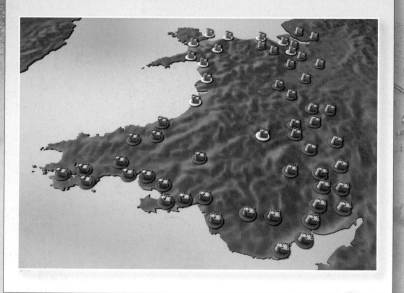

Hornwork *The outer defenses included a walled enclosure called a hornwork. This may have been intended as the local townsfolk's place of refuge during a siege.*

Island fortress

Gilbert de Clare had witnessed the six-month siege of Kenilworth Castle, England, in 1265–6, and was impressed at how well the water defenses had worked there. For his own castle he selected a site by a stream, which he then used to create a vast fortified dam to defend the castle by water.

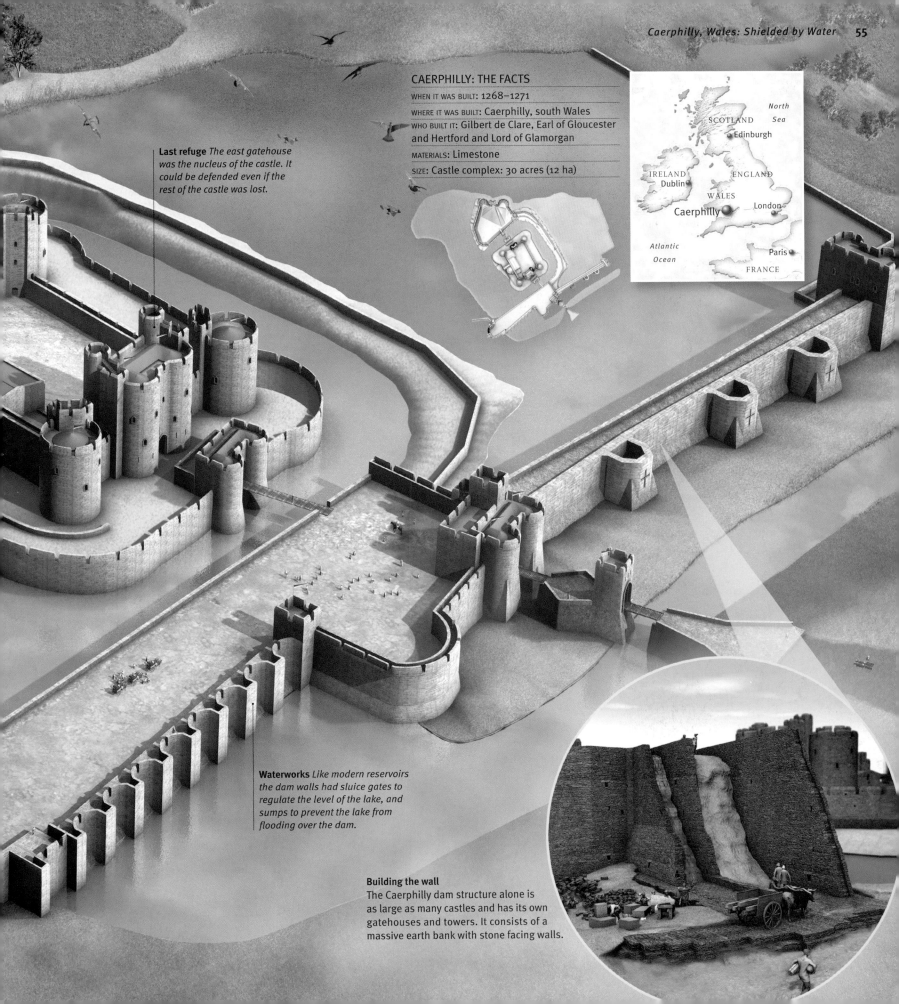

Last refuge *The east gatehouse was the nucleus of the castle. It could be defended even if the rest of the castle was lost.*

CAERPHILLY: THE FACTS

WHEN IT WAS BUILT: 1268–1271

WHERE IT WAS BUILT: Caerphilly, south Wales

WHO BUILT IT: Gilbert de Clare, Earl of Gloucester and Hertford and Lord of Glamorgan

MATERIALS: Limestone

SIZE: Castle complex: 30 acres (12 ha)

Waterworks *Like modern reservoirs the dam walls had sluice gates to regulate the level of the lake, and sumps to prevent the lake from flooding over the dam.*

Building the wall
The Caerphilly dam structure alone is as large as many castles and has its own gatehouses and towers. It consists of a massive earth bank with stone facing walls.

Mont-Saint-Michel, France

Castle in the Sea

Mont-Saint-Michel is a rocky tidal island just off the coast of Normandy in northern France. There has been an abbey on the island since about the year 708. Even without walls, the sea made the site secure, but its strategic location encouraged the monks and the kings of France to fortify the island like a castle. Throughout the Middle Ages, the abbey expanded and new buildings were built above the old ones (which survived as basements and cellars). Lower down the rock, houses and workshops of the abbey's servants grew into a little town, protected by strong walls and by the sea, which twice a day surrounded the island.

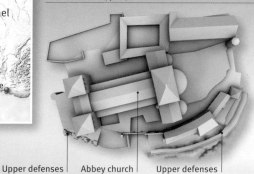

MONT-SAINT-MICHEL: THE FACTS

WHEN IT WAS BUILT: Abbey established 708, main fortifications constructed 1420s

WHERE IT WAS BUILT: Normandy, France

WHO BUILT IT: Order of Saint Benedict

MATERIALS: Granite

SIZE: 10 acres (4 ha)

Upper defenses | Abbey church | Upper defenses

Under attack

During the Hundred Years' War between France and England (which actually lasted 116 years, from 1337 to 1453), Mont-Saint-Michel was besieged by the English for several years. Fortunately for the French, the tide prevented close attack, and the English guns were too far off to be effective.

Besieged at sea

Ships at this time were small and unstable, but a small English fleet was able to blockade the island until driven off by a rival fleet of French ships.

Blast from the past *Cannons of this period were made from iron tubes fastened together. They were likely to explode if the gunpowder was poorly measured.*

Lonely campaign *The English army was small, with only a few hundred men. They found it hard to besiege the island and protect themselves against French attacks from inland.*

Risky business
Mont-Saint-Michel has long been an important site of religious pilgrimage, but crossing the tidal flats could be a treacherous journey. This drawing from a French manuscript of the 1400s shows the Virgin Mary saving a pregnant lady from drowning when cut off by the tide.

Closer to God *A village (most of which still survives) was squeezed onto platforms cut into the side of the rock.*

Church on the hill *The abbey church stood on an artificial platform, below which lay dining rooms, dormitories, kitchens, and storerooms.*

Fort Tombelaine
The English built a small timber castle on an island called Tombelaine a little way beyond Mont-Saint-Michel. About 90 soldiers stayed there, assisting in the siege.

Village alight *In 1433 the English artillery managed to set fire to some of the houses. This was the cue to launch a massive assault on the island, but the attackers were driven back, and the siege was ended.*

Barricade *The defensive walls were not high, but in combination with the sea, they proved a sufficient barrier.*

AD 1500

c. 1459: RECONSTRUCTION

AD 1400

AD 1300

1220s:
CENTRAL
KEEP BUILT

AD 1200

AD 1100

AD 1000

DRACULA: MYTH AND REALITY

Vlad III was ruler of Walachia, in Romania, three times between 1448 and 1476. His enemies were the Turks, who tried to control the region, and his noblemen, who resisted his rule. Personally cruel, he enjoyed the executions of thousands of his subjects and became known as Vlad Tepas Dracula (Vlad the Impaler, Son of the Dragon). The writer Bram Stoker took the name Dracula for his novel, but the character of Count Dracula has very little in common with Vlad III.

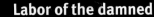

Appetite for horror
This German print from about 1500 shows Vlad III enjoying lunch among his impaled victims.

Face of a monster
This portrait is one of the earliest depictions of Vlad III, painted a few years after his death.

Labor of the damned
When Vlad III came to power in 1456, he quickly had almost all the noble families of his principality impaled because he blamed them for the murder of his father and brother. He kept a few fit nobles alive and used them as slaves to rebuild Poenari. It is said that they worked until their clothes fell off their backs.

Poenari, Romania
Dracula's Castle

Poenari Castle, high in the mountains of Romania, was first built in about 1220 but fell into ruin. When Vlad III became prince of Walachia in 1456, he decided to have the castle rebuilt as a home and refuge. The castle was a simple, narrow, walled courtyard with towers and a hall, built partially of stone and partially of brick. It occupied a small space on top of a craggy peak surrounded by cliffs. Though now it is in ruins, it is still possible to see the chambers and hall used by Vlad III. According to legend, his first wife threw herself off the cliff to escape capture by the Turks, while Vlad III escaped through a secret tunnel.

POENARI: THE FACTS

WHEN IT WAS BUILT: **1220s (central keep), rebuilt and expanded c. 1459**

WHERE IT WAS BUILT: **Făgăraş Mountains, Romania**

WHO BUILT IT: **Vlad III**

MATERIALS: **Stone and bricks**

SIZE: **210 by 40 feet (65 x 12 m)**

Original keep

Vlad III's additions

Countries and Castles

England

Dover

1 DOVER, KENT

Begun just before the Norman conquest, and kept in defensive repair until 1945, Dover Castle displays the styles of all periods of castle building.

2 RICHMOND, NORTH YORKSHIRE

A courtyard and hall design of c. 1080, with a giant keep added c. 1170.

Stirling

Scotland

3 STIRLING, STIRLING

A medieval castle rebuilt c. 1500 and now spectacularly restored to its original state.

4 BOTHWELL, LANARKSHIRE

A large castle, with huge keep, built in the early 1200s and rebuilt on a smaller scale after the Wars of Scottish Independence.

Caernarfon

Wales

5 CAERNARFON, GWYNEDD

This was largest and most expensive of Edward I's castles, built to resemble the walls of the city of Constantinople. It formed the administrative center of the new English kingdom of Wales.

6 MANORBIER, PEMBROKESHIRE

A beautiful castle, with 1100s tower, hall, and other more recent buildings inside a courtyard overlooking a little harbor.

Blarney

Ireland

7 BLARNEY, CORK

A giant tower house of the early 1400s,

set in a courtyard. Blarney is famous for the Blarney Stone, which is reputed to give the "gift of the gab" to all those who kiss it.

8 CARRICKFERGUS, ANTRIM

A well-preserved Norman castle built c. 1200, as part of the English conquest of Ireland.

Gaillard

France

9 GAILLARD, NORMANDY

A strong castle above the Seine, built to protect the approach to Rouen and Normandy. It was constructed in two years by Richard the Lionheart, 1196–8.

10 LOCHES, INDRE-ET-LOIRE

A tall keep of c. 1020–30, surrounded by late 1100s castle. It was built within a heavily fortified city that included a palatial house used by French kings.

Gravensteen

Belgium

11 GRAVENSTEEN, GHENT

A massive castle built 1180 and used as seat of the counts of Flanders.

12 BEERSEL, BRUSSELS

Beersel was built between 1300 and 1310 to defend Brussels, and rebuilt in brick in 1489, with early artillery ports in the massive towers.

Wartburg

Germany

13 WARTBURG, THURINGIA

A castle built in the mid 1100s, enclosing buildings (including a Romanesque palace) built up to the 1600s.

14 MARKSBURG, RHEINLAND-PFALZ

Marksburg was begun in 1117 and remains almost perfectly preserved in its medieval state.

Hochosterwitz

Austria

15 HOCHOSTERWITZ, CARINTHIA

A strong medieval castle (first mentioned in 860) continuously fortified until it became a palace in the 1500s.

16 FALKENSTEIN, LOWER AUSTRIA

A castle built on a high peak in 1050, it remained a fortress until dismantled in the 1600s.

Alcázar de Segovia

Spain

17 ALCÁZAR DE SEGOVIA, CASTILE-LEON

This castle on a hill was first constructed by the Moors and was extensively rebuilt in the 1400s and 1800s. It was home to several medieval kings of Spain.

18 ALJAFERÍA PALACE, ARAGON

This huge castle served as a palace, garrison fortress, and military school for about a thousand years from its construction in the 800s.

Castelvecchio

Italy

19 CASTELVECCHIO, VENETO

A double courtyard fortress built in the 1350s to defend and control the city of Verona. It was in use until 1925.

20 VOLTERRA, TUSCANY

A massive castle built on the site of a pre-Roman Etruscan city.

Acrocorinth

Greece

21 ACROCORINTH, PELOPONNESE

This ancient citadel was first built in about 700 BC. It was rebuilt several times and continuously fortified until the 1500s.

22 MISTRAS, PELOPONNESE

Begun in 1249, this castle on a rock overlooks the deserted city of Mistras, which has ruined palaces and twenty churches.

Nyborg

Denmark

23 NYBORG, FYN

A brick-built castle of the 1300s, rebuilt as a royal palace in the 1500s, and the site for 200 years of the assembly of Danish nobles.

24 KRONBORG, HOVEDSTADEN

A spacious late medieval palace with a massive artillery fort built around it in the 1500s and 1600s, this is the site of the castle of Elsinore, made famous by Shakespeare's *Hamlet*.

Bohus

Norway

25 BOHUS, BOHUSLÄN

Now in Sweden, this fortress was built in 1308 by the Norwegians on their frontier and was kept in defense until the mid-1600s, with artillery bastions.

26 CHRISTIANSØ, KRISTIANSAND

This fortress was begun in 1635 and was still in use in the 1940s as an artillery fort overlooking the sea.

Kalmar

27 Sweden

KALMAR, SMÅLAND

Kalmar was begun in the 1100s and rebuilt in the 1280s. In the 1500s it was restored as a royal palace.

28 MALMÖHUS, SCANIA

This castle in the city of Malmö was first built in 1434 and then demolished in the early 1500s. A new castle was built in its place in the 1530s by King Christian III of Denmark.

Karlštejn

Czech Republic

29 **KARLŠTEJN, CENTRAL BOHEMIA**

Karlštejn was built after 1348 by the Holy Roman Emperor, and included a great tower and palace.

Orava

Slovakia

31 **ORAVA, ŽILINA**

This castle built on a rock in the 1200s is one of the best-preserved castles in Slovakia.

Wawel

Poland

33 **WAWEL, KRAKOW**

This fortified palace was built in the 1500s on a hill which had been used as the seat of government since the 1000s.

Roumeli Hissar

Turkey

35 **ROUMELI HISSAR, ISTANBUL**

This castle was built near the Bosphorus to protect the city of Constantinople and instill fear in the local populace.

Bran

Romania

30 **BRAN, BRAȘOV COUNTY**

Bran Castle was built by the Knights of the Teutonic Order in 1212. It is promoted to tourists as "Dracula's Castle" and has been used a location for Dracula films.

Buda

Hungary

32 **BUDA, PEST COUNTY**

The original fortified medieval Buda Castle was destroyed in a siege in 1686. It was subsequently rebuilt in the Baroque style.

Pskov

Russia

34 **PSKOV, PSKOV OBLAST**

This fortress protected the capital of the medieval Pskov Republic. It was besieged over 40 times in its history, only two times successfully.

Citadel of Saladin

Syria

36 **CITADEL OF SALADIN, LATAKIA**

Formerly known as Saone, this massive Knights Hospitaller castle was built on a strategic site that has been fortified for over two thousand years.

Glossary

archer A soldier skilled in using the bow and arrow.

armorer A skilled metalworker who specialized in making armor.

artillery Originally, the name given to all machines of war, including catapults. Later, it came to mean cannons and other weapons that fire missiles with gunpowder.

battlements The defensive screen at the top of a castle wall, normally arranged with tall sections called merlons, separated by gaps called crenels. Defenders could fire at attackers through the crenels while being protected by the merlons.

blacksmith A worker who forged and shaped objects in iron. Making horseshoes was the blacksmith's main occupation.

catapult Any of a number of types of missile-throwing machines, common from Roman times onward. Catapults used throwing arms powered by giant bowstrings, counterweights, or the tension of twisted hemp or leather. They were largely replaced by cannons in the 1400s. See *trebuchet* and *mangonel*.

chain mail Armor made by hammering small circles of iron together to produce an interlocked and flexible coat. Chain mail was resistant to swords and axes but offered less protection against arrows.

chivalry From the French word for "horse," chivalry was the way of life desired by knights. It combined honor with ability in battle, skill in riding, generosity in victory, and good manners in social relations.

coat of arms Designs, painted on shields or sewn or painted on clothes and flags, used to distinguish one knight from another. Important marriages were shown by combining two or more coats of arms into a single design.

concentric castle A type of castle with two rings of defensive walls. Defenders on the higher inner walls could fire arrows at the enemy over parts of the lower outer walls.

crenellation A crenel is a gap in the battlement through which defenders fired; crenellation is the name given to the process of fortification.

crossbow A weapon in which the bow was placed horizontally on a handle shaped like a rifle butt. This allowed the bowstring to be pulled back by a winding gear to a much greater tension than a normal bow's. As a result crossbow arrows were fired with great force.

crusades The crusades were a series of nine wars fought from 1096 to 1291, usually sanctioned by the pope, with the goal of recapturing Jerusalem and the Holy Land from Muslim rule. Seen as a holy war, the western soldiers wore the emblem of a cross (Latin *crux*, hence "crusade") on their clothing and shields.

drawbridge A bridge across a moat or ditch that could be lowered to allow access or raised to keep enemies out.

dubbing The ceremony in which a squire became a knight. A noble or king tapped the flat of a sword on a squire's shoulders to symbolize his elevation to knighthood.

feudalism The social arrangement by which the king gave land to his lords, and they in turn to their followers, in return for their loyalty and service.

foot soldier A soldier who fought on foot, in contrast with knights and mounted men-at-arms, who rode and fought on horseback.

garrison A body of soldiers permanently employed to defend a particular castle. Most castles were garrisoned by only a few men but were defended during sieges by many more, brought in during times of war.

gatehouse A tower or towers set beside a castle gate to control entry.

hall The main reception room in a castle, used for formal events, meetings, and banquets.

heraldry The system of using symbols and patterns on knights' shields and surcoats so they could be identified in battle and tournaments. The word comes from "herald," a man who called out the names of knights at gatherings and had to be an expert at this system.

keep The largest tower of a castle, often where the lord had his living quarters. In the Middle Ages a keep was more commonly called a "donjon" or "great tower."

kingdom A state that had a king or queen at its head, also called a monarchy. Many countries today are monarchies, but their kings and queens have mostly symbolic power.

knight A skilled soldier who fought on horseback. Gradually it became a term of honor, since under the system of feudalism knights became powerful landowners.

lance A heavy wooden spear, up to 14 feet (4.3 m) long, carried by knights in battle and tournaments.

longbow A hand-drawn bow about 6 feet (1.8 m) long, introduced during the Middle Ages to improve the range and power of archery. The greatest range of these bows was 400 yards (360 m), and at close range they could penetrate plate armor.

loophole A narrow opening in a castle wall designed to make it difficult for attackers to fire in, while allowing defenders to fire out.

lord A powerful knight or noble who owned land that provided for his family, servants, and the peasants who worked the land for him. Lords often lived in castles.

machicolation A structure that projected over the top of a castle wall. Holes in the machicolation allowed defenders to fire arrows or drop missiles on attackers below.

mangonel A form of catapult which was powered by the tension of twisted ropes or leather. Mangonels were suitable for relatively small missiles, fired over short distances.

mason A man skilled in the cutting and laying of stone. The chief builder of a castle or church was known as the master mason.

minstrel A poet and musician who sang or recited while accompanying himself on a stringed instrument. Some minstrels were servants of a noble household; others traveled from place to place.

moat A ditch filled with water, used in particular to protect castles built on level sites. They prevented attackers from easily approaching the base of the castle walls either above ground or by digging below it.

Moors A group of Muslim people from northwest Africa who conquered large parts of Spain and Portugal in the early Middle Ages.

murder holes A series of openings in the roof of a vaulted space, such as an entrance passage, that allowed defenders to fire arrows or drop missiles onto attackers from above.

noble The highest class of landowners under the king in medieval society. Nobles usually came from a few dozen great families, often related to the king. Many nobles were also knights.

Normans Originally Vikings who settled in northern France in the early 900s, the Normans assimilated with the local French nobles to form a strong military society feared across Europe. They conquered England, Sicily, and parts of Italy and Ireland.

page A youth, generally the son of a knight, who was brought up to serve in a nobleman's household. Pages might be eight or nine years old, and if successful might become squires in their midteens.

parapet A barrier at the top of a wall to prevent people from falling over the edge, often capped by battlements.

peasant A term, literally "countryman" (French), that in modern English refers to the poorer farmers and laborers of the Middle Ages. Medieval words were more specific, and included "slave," "villein," "cottager," and "serf," depending on the exact status of the person described.

plate armor Armor made of plates of iron cut to fit around the body, with hinges at the joints and chain mail at the back of the knees and elbows. This provided better protection than the earlier chain-mail coats, which they largely replaced.

portcullis A heavy lattice gate of timber covered with iron raised above an entrance passage. Once lowered, it was a formidable barrier that required axes to break.

serf A farmer who was tied to the land and whose life was regulated by his lord. The word originally meant slave (Latin *servus*), but in the Middle Ages the serf had some rights, although was forbidden to leave his or her land.

siege Attacking a castle by surrounding it and preventing supplies and reinforcements from reaching those inside.

siege engine The name given to a variety of mostly wooden machines designed to break walls and demoralize defenders. They included catapults, trebuchets, and siege towers.

siege tower A massive timber tower on wheels, with ladders and fighting platforms inside, normally protected by plates or wet hides. They were designed to overlook the top of a castle's walls and to be pushed up against the walls to allow attackers to storm the castle.

squire A young man, formerly a page, who accompanied a knight and helped to maintain the knight's horses, armor, and weapons. After an apprenticeship of five or ten years, a squire might hope to become a knight.

surcoat A loose cloth coat worn above armor, to protect it from dust and rain. The surcoat was painted or embroidered with the coat of arms of the knight.

tournament A mock battle, in which knights in groups or in pairs exhibited their skills at riding and fighting. Tournaments were dangerous, but the victor would expect to win fame and wealth, since the losers' weapons and armor were normally awarded to the winner.

trebuchet The largest of the missile-throwing siege machines. A trebuchet consisted of a hinged beam with a heavy counterweight on one end and a sling loaded with a heavy rock or other missile on the other. When a securing rope was released, the counterweight swung the arm violently up, and slung the missile against the target.

turret A small tower built on top of a larger tower or wall and used as a lookout.

undermining A siege tactic in which miners dug tunnels underneath the foundations of a wall or tower. When the tunnel was complete, straw and oil-soaked materials were set alight to burn the tunnel supports, and if all went according to plan, the wall above would crack and might collapse.

ward A courtyard or enclosure of a castle. Concentric castles typically had an inner ward completely surrounded by an outer ward.

Index

Credits

The publisher thanks Alexandra Cooper for her contribution, and Puddingburn for the index.

ILLUSTRATIONS
Front cover Moonrunner Design (main), GODD.com (supports);
back cover GODD.com
Spellcraft Studio e.K. 38–39, 46–47; **All other illustrations** GODD.com
(Markus Junker, Rolf Schröter, Patrick Tilp, Robert Keller, Julian Krause)

MAPS
Map Illustrations

PHOTOGRAPHS
Key t=top; l=left; r=right; tl=top left; tcl=top center left; tc=top center;
tcr=top center right; tr=top right; cl=center left; c=center; cr=center right;
b=bottom; bl=bottom left; bcl=bottom center left; bc=bottom center;
bcr=bottom center right; br=bottom right

AA=The Art Archive; APL=Australian Picture Library; BA=Bridgeman Art
Library; CBT=Corbis; iS=iStock; MEPL=Mary Evans Picture Library; PIC=
The Picture Desk; PL=photolibrary.com

8bl APL; **10**br APL; **11**tr AA; **30**tr BA; **32**tr PIC; **37**tr PL; **40**bl BA; **47**br APL;
48bc PL; bcl, bl CBT; **53**tr AA; **57**tl MEPL; **58**tl MEPL; tr BA; **60–61** iS